Monkey Business

HOWLER MONKEYS

Gillian Gosman

PowerKiDS
press
New York

Published in 2012 by The Rosen Publishing Group, Inc.
29 East 21st Street, New York, NY 10010

First Edition

Editor: Jennifer Way
Book Design: Kate Laczynski

Photo Credits: Cover, p. 1 © Juan Carlos Muñoz/age fotostock; p. 4 Stockbyte/Thinkstock; p. 5 David Tipling/Getty Images; pp. 6, 8, 9, 13, 15 (left) Shutterstock.com; p. 7 Tier Und Naturfotografie J & C Sohns/Getty Images; pp. 8, 16, 17 Visuals Unlimited, Inc./Thomas Marent/Getty Images; pp. 10–11 © www.iStockphoto.com/Darren Deans; p. 12 Anup Shah/Photodisc/Thinkstock; pp. 14, 20, 21 Tom Brakefield/Stockbyte/Thinkstock; p. 15 (right) © www.iStockphoto.com/Erik Gauger; pp. 18–19 © Chico Sanchez/age fotostock; p. 22 iStockphoto/Thinkstock.

Library of Congress Cataloging-in-Publication Data

Gosman, Gillian.
 Howler monkeys / by Gillian Gosman. — 1st ed.
     p. cm. — (Monkey business)
 Includes index.
 ISBN 978-1-4488-5019-8 (library binding) — ISBN 978-1-4488-5171-3 (pbk.) — ISBN 978-1-4488-5172-0 (6-pack)
 1. Howler monkeys—Juvenile literature. I. Title.
 QL737.P915G67 2012
 599.8'55—dc22
                          2010047860

Manufactured in the United States of America

CPSIA Compliance Information: Batch #WS11PK: For Further Information contact Rosen Publishing, New York, New York at 1-800-237-9932

Contents

MEET THE HOWLER MONKEY

A howl is a long, wild cry, and that is just what howler monkeys are known for. In the early morning and late afternoon, howler monkeys come together to make some noise.

A few monkeys begin to howl, and soon all of the males in the **troop**, or group, have joined in.

Howler monkeys spend a great deal of the day resting in trees.

Males from other troops answer their howls. Why do howler monkeys howl? To let other monkey troops know that they should stay away because this area is taken!

FUN FACT

The sound of howler monkeys howling can be heard up to 3 miles (5 km) away.

his black howler monkey is letting loose with its distinctive
ll. This loud call helps it find other males in its troop and
ll monkeys from other troops to stay away!

NEW WORLD MONKEY

Map of Central America and South America

BELIZE
HONDURAS
GUATEMALA
NICARAGUA
EL SALVADOR
COSTA RICA
PANAMA
VENEZUELA
GUYANA
SURINAME
FRENCH GUIANA
COLOMBIA
ECUADOR
PERU
BOLIVIA
BRAZIL
CHILE
PARAGUAY
ARGENTINA
URUGUAY

Howler monkeys are **New World** monkeys. This is because they live in the New World. The New World is North America and South America. Howler monkeys are most common in the South

This map shows Central Ameri and South America. Howler monkeys live in tropical rain forests in this part of the world

American countries of Brazil, Bolivia, Argentina, and Paraguay.

New World monkeys are known for their noses. Their noses are long and have one large nostril, or opening, on either side. Some New World monkeys have **prehensile** tails, or tails that can hold on to tree branches.

THE BIGGEST MONKEY

There are several **species** of howler monkeys. There are also many howler monkey subspecies. A subspecies is a grouping within a species. Howlers are the largest of the New World monkeys.

Howler monkeys can grow to be 3 feet (1 m) long and weigh 22 pounds (10 kg). Their powerful prehensile tails add to their

The body of an adult red howler monkey is between 19 to 28 inches (48–71 cm) long. Adult females are generally a little smaller. Its prehensile tail doubles the howler monkey's body length!

total length. Howler monkeys have long, thick hair that may be black, brown, or red. Their faces are hairless. They have full beards covering their large throats. These house the extra large **vocal cords**, which they use to make their howls.

ere is an adult howler monkey and a younger howler monkey.

TOGETHER AS A TROOP

Howler monkeys live in groups, called troops. Howler monkey troops do not get along with other troops. If monkeys from different troops get too close to one another, they often fight!

There can be between 3 and 20 monkeys in a troop. Each troop is lead by a head male, the monkey that is the strongest and smartest of the group. Most troops have between one

Here is a group of howler monkeys calling out to other monkeys from their perch in a tree at a zoo.

and three adult males, between two and four adult females, and a group of babies and young monkeys. However, some troops are made up of only adult males.

FUN FACT

A male from an all-male troop might decide to fight with the head male of a family. Whichever monkey wins the fight will take charge of the females and the young.

A WALK IN THE TREES!

Howler monkeys live in the wet and dry forests of South America. They can hold on to tree branches with their prehensile tails, allowing them to move from tree to tree.

Arboreal monkeys like the howler monkey also use their tails to balance while they move around in trees.

This is a common way for howler monkeys to sit when they are resting or sleeping. Its legs and tail keep the monkey balanced and safe from falling out of the tree.

Howler monkeys hardly ever come down to the ground. They spend their time in the forest **canopy**, or the highest tree branches. They eat in the trees, play in the trees, and sleep in the trees. Animals that spend a great deal of their time in the high branches of trees are called **arboreal**. They move from tree to tree to look for food.

LOVING LEAVES

Howler monkeys are **herbivores**, meaning they eat only plants. They eat leaves, fruits, and flowers that grow high above the ground.

Young leaves are the most **nutritious**, or healthy, and the easiest to eat. Fruits and flowers are harder to find. Howler monkeys

Howler monkeys eat mostly leaves, but they are known to eat birds' eggs, too.

especially enjoy figs, sweet brown fruits with tiny seeds. When no fruits or flowers can be found, howler monkeys can live for two or three weeks on leaves alone.

Howler monkeys eat both young and mature leaves. On some trees, they must be careful of the mature leaves, which contain toxins, or chemicals that can make the monkeys sick.

Having a prehensile tail frees up the howler monkey's hands and feet to get to harder-to-reach leaves.

MONKEYING AROUND

Howler monkeys are **diurnal**, or active during the day. They still spend most of their day resting, though. They find a nice branch and take long naps. They wake to eat and to play. They move slowly because they are so large, though.

The howler monkey's leafy diet is low in energy. That is one reason they stop to rest many times during the day.

Howler monkeys are **quadrupeds**, meaning they walk on four legs. Their strong tails are like fifth legs. They have no hair on their tails' undersides so that they can hold tree branches easily. This also gives the monkeys strength and balance.

The hairless pad on the underside of the howler monkey's prehensile tail has lines on it, like those on the palm of your hand.

MOM AND DAD MONKEY

The head male leads the troop for between two and three years. During this time, he will **mate** with the females of the troop and father as many as 18 babies.

Male and female monkeys come together to mate high in the trees. The female makes faces at the male with her mouth and tongue. The male pays special attention to her, sometimes following her around for days. He

Here is a female black howler monkey and her baby. Female howler monkeys can mate at around three years old. Male howler monkeys can mate at around three and a half years old.

touches his nose to hers and rubs his neck and back on nearby branches. He leaves his scent on the branches, letting other male monkeys know that he is in charge.

FUN FACT

Howler monkeys come together to mate when they are between three and five years old.

BABY TIME!

Howler monkeys generally have one baby at a time. The female howler monkey carries the unborn baby for six months before giving birth.

The newborn howler will hold on tightly to its mother's belly fur for the first few weeks. Then it

Baby howler monkeys start to eat some leaves when they are about three weeks old. They drink their mothers' milk throughout their first year, though.

As baby howler monkeys grow, they play and explore the world around them. That way, they get to know other members of their troop and how to find food.

will learn to ride on its mother's back. For the first 6 to 10 months of its life, it will travel with its mother in this way. By the time it is one year old, it will have learned how to find food for itself and will soon leave its parents' troop to start life as an adult.

FUN FACT

A female howler monkey will give birth to a new baby every 18 to 24 months. In the wild, a howler monkey might live to be 15 years old.

COMING TO THE END?

People have been no friend to the howler monkey. Across South America, howler monkeys are hunted for their meat and their fur. People have also destroyed much of the **rain forests** where howler monkeys live. Each troop of howler monkeys needs a large piece of land to call its own.

Rain forests have been cut down throughout the howler monkey's range. This destroys its habitat and has led to howler monkeys becoming rare in many places.

As people cut down the rain forests, the monkeys are forced to live on smaller and smaller pieces of land. There is not enough food or space for them. Scientists have said that some species or populations of howler monkeys may become **extinct** in the next 35 years.

Glossary

arboreal (ahr-BOR-ee-ul) Having to do with trees.

canopy (KA-nuh-pee) The highest tree branches in a forest.

diurnal (dy-UR-nul) Active during the daytime.

extinct (ik-STINGKT) No longer existing.

herbivores (ER-buh-vorz) Animals that eat only plants.

mate (MAYT) To come together to make babies.

New World (NOO WURLD) North America and South America.

nutritious (noo-TRIH-shus) Healthy.

prehensile (pree-HEN-sul) Able to grab by wrapping around.

quadrupeds (KWAH-druh-pedz) Animals with four feet.

rain forests (RAYN FOR-ests) Thick forests that receive a large amount of rain during the year.

species (SPEE-sheez) One kind of living thing. All people are one species.

troop (TROOP) A group of animals.

vocal cords (VOH-kul KORDZ) Two small bands of body tissue that stretch across the voice box and move to make sounds.

Index

Web Sites

Due to the changing nature of Internet links, PowerKids Press has developed an online list of Web sites related to the subject of this book. This site is updated regularly. Please use this link to access the list: www.powerkidslinks.com/monk/howler/